BEAUTIFUL MOTION

Other volumes in the series:

The Morse Poetry Prize
Edited by Guy Rotella

DANA ROESER

Beautiful Motion

THE 2004 MORSE
POETRY PRIZE
SELECTED AND
INTRODUCED BY
ELLEN BRYANT VOIGT

Northeastern University Press
BOSTON

Northeastern University Press

Library of Congress Cataloging-in-Publication Data
Roeser, Dana, 1953–
    Beautiful Motion / Dana Roeser ; selected and introduced by Ellen Bryant Voigt
        p. cm. — (The 2004 Morse Poetry Prize)
    ISBN 1-55553-622-0 (pbk. : alk. paper)
    I. Voigt, Ellen Bryant. II. Title. III. Morse Poetry Prize ; 2004.
    PS3618.O38B43 2004
    811'.6—dc22   2004014779

Designed by Ann Twombly

Composed in Weiss. Printed and bound by Edwards Brothers, Inc, Lillington,
North Carolina. The paper is EB Natural, an acid-free stock.

MANUFACTURED IN THE UNITED STATES OF AMERICA
08   07   06   05   04   5   4   3   2   1

For Don, Eleanor, and Lucy

ACKNOWLEDGMENTS

Thanks to the editors of the following publications, in which these poems, sometimes in different versions, first appeared:

Another Chicago Magazine:	"In Praise of Annuals"
The Antioch Review:	"My Mother Is Magic"
descant:	"Land of the Lotus Eaters: Sea Island, Georgia" (winner of the 2003 Betsy Colquitt Award)
Hiram Poetry Review:	"November 15, Before the Frost"
Indiana Review:	"Jesus at the Help Desk" (second place, *Indiana Review* 2003 Poetry Prize)
The Iowa Review:	"Ars Domestica," "3 A.M.: Put Pedro to Sleep"
The Laurel Review:	"Charlie Butterworth Is in My Soul"
Limestone:	"Making Out"
The Literary Review:	"Hot Flash"
The Massachusetts Review:	"Glitter & Shine"
Northwest Review:	"Glass Breaking: February Meditation—Ragdale Foundation, Lake Forest, Illinois"
Passages North:	"Something Sharp and the River," "The Bill Irwin Memorial"
Poem:	"Suck and Purl"
Pool:	"Beautiful Motion," "Low Horizon"
Shade:	"The Water Table"
Snake Nation Review:	"Abigail"
The Spoon River Poetry Review:	"His Hands like Warm Earth"
The Virginia Quarterly Review:	"Under Water"

"Ars Domestica" appeared on *Poetry Daily* (www.poems.com) on September 27, 1999.

"3 A.M.: Put Pedro to Sleep" and "Charlie Butterworth Is in My Soul" were reprinted in the on-line journal *The Melic Review* (Fall 2003).

For their generous help with these poems/this book, I would like to thank Bruce Beasley, Hilene Flanzbaum, Jacqueline Osherow, Donald Platt, and Judith Taylor. For their sensitive reading and criticism of this book in manuscript form, my heartfelt thanks to Ellen Bryant Voigt and Guy Rotella, Series Editor.

Special thanks to Donald Revell.

I would also like to express my gratitude to Eavan Boland, Christopher Burske, George Garrett, Patricia Henley, Tony Hoagland, Josie Kearns, David Dodd Lee, the late Larry Levis, Norman Minnick, Gregory Orr, Katharine Rodier, Keith Smith, Lisa Russ Spaar, Janet Sylvester, Betsy Fogelman Tighe, and Charles Wright. And many thanks to my parents, the late Dana Davis Roeser and Erwin Roeser, my brother John and his family, my brother Douglas, the late Eleanor Beckham, and Martha Platt. I am indebted to my daughters, Eleanor and Lucy, and especially, my husband, Donald Platt, for their generous love and support.

I would like to acknowledge the following artists' colonies who granted residencies that aided in the completion of this book: the Ragdale Foundation, Mary Anderson Center, and Virginia Center for the Creative Arts. Thanks also to the Post-Graduate Writers' Conference at Vermont College, RopeWalk Writers Retreat, Purdue University, and Butler University.

Contents

Introduction

According to Robert Frost, "There are only three things, after all, that a poem must reach: the eye, the ear, and what we may call the heart or the mind. It is most important of all to reach the heart of the reader. And the surest way to reach the heart is through the ear." Dana Roeser knows this down to the bone: the evidence abounds in *Beautiful Motion*.

Never mind that Frost was famously grumpy about free verse, and that Roeser is fearlessly inventive with open form. In her poems—with their "perky" lineation, their "expensive white space," their "name, dates, places//and other numbers"—the pace is certainly faster, the temperature higher, the speaker more immediate, closer to Plath than to Frost. First reading this volume, one might even think Williams a more likely precursor, by way of Creeley's relentless enjambment, perhaps, or Bidart's hyperbole and formal drama. But while Roeser's rhythms are a long way indeed from Frost's iambs (and in part a critique of them), her short, interrupted, syncopated lines form the same sort of "crossed swords" as his fixed meter, around which idiom dances so nimbly.

Her chief tools are, like Frost's, diction and syntax:

> As when a plane
> takes off, doesn't fly very
>   high, then lands,
> or doesn't, gets
>   hung up in
> a ski cable, a
>   mountain, I have
> low trajectory. . . .
>   What's the
> big deal about

success anyway? Isn't
that just a myth? Yet
    I see the
things I set out to do
    back off, flatten
out.

The lexicon is drawn from speech, thoroughly and endearing-
ly contaminated in the postmodern soup by advertising, self-help,
science, pop media, and higher ed; "dinners, lunches, clothes, cap-
puccinos" jostle alongside "some ancient cornice in Malta" or "the
meaning of 'brackish.'" This is the world as we know it now, and it
crowds every page of this book—democratically, with equal anxiety
and disappointment, since Roeser's violently enjambed lines and
edgy tercets refuse to honor one detail over another, the "dumb blue
spikes of ajuga" over "a freshly baked loaf of bread/still in its cello-
phane."
    Meanwhile, what Frost would recognize as "vital sentences"—
the "sound of sense"—propel Roeser's poems down the page. In-
exorable, they drive us across line breaks into the wall of another
structural jump-cut—the perfect musical score for her restless, allu-
sive mind, her complex emotional range:

        I was like
    that guy out in Utah, Richard
Worthington, who thought his unborn children—
    he'd had 12—were all
waiting up there to be born—his wife
    was tired and went to get
her tubes tied, when he came in
    with a gun—the eggs
waiting to hatch like
    Mexican jumping beans,
torturing him. Eleanor was not
    ready for another dog

after what we went through
    with Pedro. Shirley needs
holy water, consecrated oil, bad.
    I was going to be
an exotic flower in suburbia! Ha!

Most of what these poems record is dilemma: intractable, mis-
takenly wished-for, overwhelming, unsolaced by the old Romantic
verities extracted from nature or self-awareness. This work avoids
high-toned ambitions, the smug or "literary," the merely pretty or
sonorous, trumpeted triumph or wisdom or convincing reconcilia-
tion. Pricked and pulled by doubt, envy, tenderness, self-critique,
grief, and domestic claustrophobia, Roeser's protagonist, like the sly
poet herself, seems to defeat convention by earnest failure at it.

Yet these accessible, energetic poems are full of quiet insight,
usually presented as minor capitulation, major consequences left
understated:

    That's it, like
a light on
    or a light off,
like that tree glorying
    in the damp
coolness out there—
    you know how
they mysteriously
    brighten in the rain—
then shedding, still
    glorious,
while I sweat it
    out inside
then boom
    the tree
is indistinguishable
    from the others,

the yard, the gray
    sky, leaf
rot, no
    longer standing
out.

What reaches the reader's heart—through the ear, as Frost said
it would—is tone: varied, candid, pitch-perfect, inscribed by syntax
and lineation. In her rich, undeceived catalogs of the world, we hear
one "soul . . . taken by surprise," one immutably human,

    dysthymic, hyperthymic,
sex-crazed, hypomanic,
    money-throwing,
neurasthenic
    soul
rattling in its
    cage, in its
blankets and heaters
    and down
quilts, wrapped in
    layers of flannel
and wool, wearing socks,
    a fleece hat.

Its sounds are indelible, and without precedent.

ELLEN BRYANT VOIGT

I

"the key to this life is surprise"

"I'm sure tomorrow I'll feel joy again"

"we keep women's ashes in jars on
the mantel"

"it's hard to be who I am in my new
life"

"their insistence on being all about process
not consummation"

"the world is smeared w/ vaseline"

Ars Domestica

The key to this life is
            surprise. Don't say
my whole life is spent
            trying to reunite
socks. Say instead,
            surprise! Here is Eleanor's
white cotton undershirt.
            Surprise! My husband slept
in the living room; he's in
            a bad mood. Surprise!
Eleanor spilled lemonade
            over the coffee table
and onto the Persian rug.
            Surprise, it's warm
and looks like rain and
            little red berries are
showing up on the blushing
            dogwood leaves.
There's a bit of
            laundry accumulating in the
laundry room: a light pile!
            a dark pile! and a cold
wash pile! Surprise!
            Eleanor coughed so
hard this morning she
            gagged and threw up
in the toilet. Not: Every morning
            and evening she does
this. Not: Every time she comes off
            medication, she gets sick
and runs a fever in precisely
            three days. Not: Every time
she gets a full glass

of lemonade . . . .
Not, I am getting older and
        will never look a) young
b) fresh c) thin, again.
        No. Surprise! My face
looks rumpled and tired—
        I'm sure tomorrow I'll
look young again. No.

        Surprise! I seem a little
plump today, can't seem to close
        a size 16 around
my waist. See above.
        I'm so surprised—my
roots keep growing in dark
        with gray streaks!
I'm sure I'll have the pale
        yellow hair of my
childhood any minute.

        I'm so surprised. Lucy wants to
a) nurse again b) eat again c) put
        a foreign object
into her mouth again.
        Mix up the burners! Put the rice
pilaf on the front burner
        to cool, move
the pasta water behind it
        to heat—then,
turn on the wrong burner!
        Presto! The smoke alarm!
Hand stuck on the horn!
        The pilaf soldered
to the pan! What a wonderful
        surprise! The whole family
has to run out of the house

                    into the cloud that has
just landed and is lying
                    in the yellow grass
of the front yard.

Low Horizon

As when a plane
takes off, doesn't fly very
        high, then lands,
or doesn't, gets
        hung up in
a ski cable, a
        mountain, I have
low trajectory. A
        curve that doesn't
get very high before
        it comes back down. So
I avoid the spectacular
        crashes, I follow my
instruments carefully to
        fly in fog. Like
Phaëthon, I scorch the
        earth with my
low achievements.
                    What's the
big deal about
        success anyway? Isn't
that just a myth? Yet
        I see the
things I set out to do
        back off, flatten
out. Suze Orman
        on TV: "The Courage
to Be Rich." How about
        the courage to
balance one's check-
        book, the courage
to *make* money, *any*
        money?

Suze Orman's
hair sticks up like
        a helmet; she
has that predatory,
        animal smile
like she's just torn
        into a piece of
raw meat. What
        can you get out
of your IRA
        before you're
59 (what can you
        put in)?
Save $105,000 for just
        $253 a month—
own your own house outright!—
        and the
prenuptial agreement,
        90%
of divorces (1 in 2
        couples will divorce)
are caused by arguments
        over . . . . Whoa-ho!
Hello! My spouse and
        his baby-buffalo, pit-bull
therapist are leering at
        me again.
My mother sits at the
        dinner table
and chats with my
        husband—who
on St. John's Wort and a steady
        job is borderline
expansive. . . . I'm
        flying through

7

the fog of mismatched
        dinnerware (at least
I found some *clean*, if motley,
        napkins), the rust
on the knives, the
        huge stain on the rug
a few steps away
        that seemed to come
out of nowhere—I'm so
        busy flying
through the fog, the fumes
        of the mosquito
truck, of the hideous
        paneled wainscoting
in the living room,
        the permanently glazed
and clouded double-
        pane windows, the
cardboard boxes in the hall
        filled with stuff from
the last time I had the carpet
        cleaned, the heaped
laundry basket, my white
        shirt back from
the cleaners—I can see
        the tamari flying
toward it! While my
        mother and husband joyfully
beat around the bush doing
        the self-satisfied
"Aren't we doing well
        at seeming
close, at saying
        nothing?" dance, I'm
droning through the air,

the kitchen still
smoking from
  the swordfish catching
fire under the broiler.
      <u>Why</u>
  <u>can't we</u>
<u>borrow money and</u>
   <u>remodel this</u>
<u>place right now? I'll get</u>
   <u>a clutter doctor, a</u>
<u>Feng Shui doctor,</u>
    <u>I'll get on some</u>
<u>kind of really neatnik,</u>
   <u>order-inducing meds</u> . . . .
<u>I see my house</u>
   <u>transposed on my</u>
<u>mother's and I see what</u>
   <u>she sees, what</u>
<u>she's said about my</u>
   <u>relatives, my father's</u>
<u>sisters: filth, clutter,</u> . . .
   horrors! And I fly
through desperately, a winged
   ant, a fruit bat,
a June bug that shouldn't have
   come indoors.

      Mike and Alizon live
next door, in a house
   equally appalling. Summer,
Mike spends whole days
   building and repairing
model airplanes at a long
   table in his garage,
cigarette dangling out

of his mouth. On
Saturdays, he borrows
          someone's field so he
can take out
          the plane
he's just finished
          and fly it. At the
end of the day,
          he comes back,
face dirty, animated, says
          it crashed.
                    Before he goes
back into his workbench
          to try to repair
the mangled plane, the Sisyphean
          task he loves, he
goes and sits in the wrecked
          Toyota parked in his
yard, the car he drove
          into a ditch last week, and
lights a smoke, takes
          a breather; he thinks
about Amelia Earhart and the
          Hindenburg, and other
aviation disasters,
          and all of
history's splendid
          failures.

Asthma in Summer:
Family Vacation at Virginia Beach

The oppressive night
like a blanket. Layers
    of wetness on
my bronchial tubes, my
    limbs; my
husband's body
    on top of me. I
want to walk out, to the bay,
    the ocean, to a
mountain, to a place of
    stars.
        In my dream,
men keep women's
    selves,
women's souls, in
    little jars along
the mantel, and it makes it so
    much easier. Then
the women hold the broom,
    the fork, but
not the knife. At Kokoro,
    the Japanese chef
tosses it in the air—and
    catches it.
        My children.
The sticking point.
    I remember their
babyhoods in this little
    house. Each cried to
be let into my bed. Tonight,
    the older one came
to sleep with me. Her

11

sunburn hurt. I held
her hand, then gripped
        my rosary, praying.
How will I sleep? Wanting
        to walk out
as I do, the dinners,
        the nights out,
the purple pedicure. These will
        prevent the questions.

Where does the energy
        come from? The
longest earthworm, five feet, in
        Australia, may be
energized by alluvial ooze. But
        who knows how long
it languishes under there
        waiting for a
sea change, a change in
        the upper weather,
so it can come out, move
        under the sky? A
woman found it. She dug
        for a year. She
knew it was down
        there.
                Dinners, lunches,
clothes, cappuccinos. Search
        if you want, but don't
find it. . . . I gasp for air. I
        search for that
hard, bright thing at
        night. Walking
the dog, I see my stooped
        shadow in the

streetlight—so
     like my father's.
Or jogging
     in daylight—the
hat, the lurching legs. I drive
     up to a gas station—
what a relief, a
     long blue sign with
white letters, "Self"—available
     at the pumps. Little
selves, little yellow-winged
     souls, fly around, close
enough to pull from
     the air. I rest
there, holding the nozzle,
     guiding it into
the gas tank, the hole.

3 A.M.: *Put Pedro to Sleep*

I know exactly what death looks like

    downy hills   pale green
                       tufts of cottonwood trees
    ribbon of road, ribbon of river.

The needle, long and shiny . . . .

Her breath rises and I feel for it.

She's small.
              During the apneas
                  the little pauses

she might drift   as on a hang glider

over that   landscape.

I almost pushed him down

        the cliff

    on Canyon Road
        on his last day   today

I thought about it

Pedro, companion
            of my loneliness

      my solitary glides, at night,
   over those hills.

Why do they call it

      putting to sleep?

At night
        we turn ourselves over to God.

In the spring   on the first warm
                       hot days

that force the buds open

       force purple-scented lilac
            from dun-leaved bushes

people want

       to feel the sun and air again.

They take off their shirts

then,
      their heads

with a gun, with . . . .

My baby and I keep our shirts on,

stay on this side.

Pedro scrabbles up the edge

across the stones
       in rapid water.

Pedro, ball of will
             and bites,

wagging his white-tipped tail
          when he comes to me.

He'll be put to sleep.

  At first, his rest will be very dark;

then, wisps of dawn
    will fill the house;

he'll scratch to be let out

his black and brown tank-shaped body

        will trot down the sidewalk

    his toenails will click

        his collar will jingle

an hour later

        he'll return from Smith's

as he does
            every morning

from scrounging   the dumpster

        with a whole roast chicken

    a dozen spareribs   raw or cooked

a freshly baked loaf of bread
                still in its cellophane. . . .

Under Water

The bloodshot toddler
in my daughter's swim class
        drifts again and again under
water—she *likes* it so much down there.
        She can hardly obey the requirement
to keep her hands
            on the edge of the deep end.
With her mother after class
            I've seen her breaststroke under water
several feet at a time.
        She comes up, composed,
blond bangs streaming.

        My daughter still hesitates,
even in the instructor's arms,
        refuses to go under.
I'm hoping practice will turn her
        amphibious
like the blond girl.
        At night she cries out
and comes into my bed
        and won't fall asleep again
until she has my hand.

        When I close my eyes
at what used to be my favorite time,
        the drift into speaking dreams,
the release from gravity
        and the thousand rules,
I see the child
        written up in all the papers
who at 2 1/2
        was made to switch parents.
I see her groping the new house,

the new parents,
for her old ones.
It's as though she is under water
and can't come up.

Glitter & Shine

                The rumpled sleeping bag, Pedro's,
is still on the cold floor of the
                carport. The water bowl, the cat chow
bowl, I took in. Green eyes, chocolate part-
                Labrador, skin and bones
sweetheart. Little brown dog—I found
                someone to take you. Shirley colors
her hair, blond, auburn, whatever
                comes to mind. Shirley's psychic,
sober 7 months with 2
                slips. Shirley's a healer.
Eleanor wasn't over Pedro. She was
                relieved when Brandon took
the stray. Who loved me already. Who
                met my car in the sun today
out by the mailbox. I gave her water,
                cat chow, a sunbeam, a bed—
I wish she were there now and the sun
                were shining. Bars of rain,
a little box of space and time, then all
                eternity—my girls growing
up there, saddle shoes, high-tops,
                size 3 size 4 size 13
size 1 little footsoles I massage
                then a big wild foot that
stomps by—but with those same-shaped
                toenails, their father's curved
toes. What would I have named her?
                I'm finally over the
desire to have more children.
                Or even a dog. Whole
days I go without
                cat chow, feed the cat

albacore, or forget. I thought
        possibilities would keep
multiplying like a jolly surf. Now
        it's a cheap drum machine
I fell for. Now it's garbage and garbage
        bags. It's refrigerator
hum, dripping sink—I was going to
        make them magical
over & over & over. Gild them with
        gold. Can you imagine? A
ranch house with fake bricks and
        wood grain veneer?
Shirley says that room was so full of
        evil. Lines mirrors booze
needles rock crank. Shirley
        says she ran into someone
from AA there! I was like
        that guy out in Utah, Richard
Worthington, who thought his unborn children—
        he'd had 12—were all
waiting up there to be born—his wife
        was tired and went to get
her tubes tied, when he came in
        with a gun—the eggs
waiting to hatch like
        Mexican jumping beans,
torturing him. Eleanor was not
        ready for another dog
after what we went through
        with Pedro. Shirley needs
holy water, consecrated oil, bad.
        I was going to be
an exotic flower in suburbia! Ha!
        Can you imagine? Genes
or money, either way I haven't

got them. My days made
daily by a little brown dog.
        I'm over that now. I know
that 900 dogs per week are euthanized. 60
        per month are adopted.
I'm over imagining each of the 900 as mine,
        wagging their tails, following me. I
decided to color my hair, no
        gray for me, no
yellow plastic garbage tie around
        me, thanks. Soon
I know she would bark, beg
        for food at the table,
become annoying. No more soundless puppy
        footfall, crescent toes.
I still have the smell of her
        on my
sweater. She slept in the sun,
        waited for me.
It was colder last night
        than hell. Really. Somewhere
out there, she got through it.
        I don't know
if Shirley healed Cheeko's arm
        or not. If she
jumped from bed looking for
        him when he was in California
then prayed him well when—she learned this later—
        the steel piece fell and smashed
his arm. The cat's name
        is Sparkling. We all glitter &
shine here. Or did. Eleanor and Lucy
        are not lovely-faced little mirrors
put on this earth so I can look
        but willful creatures

needing to be taught. Or Shirley's story
       about searching for a waiting room
for a woman in green so she
       could pass the message
God sent. I believe that one. I
       believe Brandon is keeping
that dog warm.

November 15, Before the Frost

This morning
I found out
    I could smell,
an acrid, shit smell,
        everywhere, in the
frying pan with the
        pancakes,
hovering around my daughter
        in her leotard,
and I
        found out about
nature—that
        it exists, that
there's an
        outdoors and that
while I've been
        indoors flat
in bed, or turning
        from side to
side, sweat
        pooling in the
collar of my
        nightie, during
the rain I've
        vaguely heard
all week roaring
        on the roof,
the gold leaves
        of the sugar maple
next door
        have been falling—
I had just noticed
        the tree before I got

sick, had said
　　　　to myself, Finally,
November whatever
　　　　and there's a dressed-
up tree! I'll bet
　　　　the whole
darn thing's down
　　　　now, since I've
come in to do
　　　　the dishes.
Yesterday I found
　　　　my journal from
four years
　　　　ago. I certainly
didn't know it
　　　　then, but I look
upon it now
　　　　as a sort of
golden age;
　　　　then it was cold
slush, but now
　　　　it's snow in the
streetlights at twilight,
　　　　the cold creeping
up the walls of the
　　　　house, the radiator
clanking. I saw him for
　　　　one hour every
other week
　　　　for three years.
He saw the same
　　　　movies I did and
talked about
　　　　the splendors
of failure. He had a son. . .

24

        I realized with a
kind of sharp pang
        my precise loss. That
my life without
        him is
unquestionably poorer.
        That's it, like
a light on
        or a light off,
like that tree glorying
        in the damp
coolness out there—
        you know how
they mysteriously
        brighten in the rain—
then shedding, still
        glorious,
while I sweat it
        out inside
then boom
        the tree
is indistinguishable
        from the others,
the yard, the gray
        sky, leaf
rot, no
        longer standing
out.

Land of the Lotus Eaters: Sea Island, Georgia

Corpses I once
        dreamt about,
at an amusement
        park, on a carousel,
somnambulent
        in the gauzy
September light, their
        skin weathered,
their eyes tumbled like
        stones by
the ocean air—imparadised
        on the seaside
patio with baby greens,
        smoked oysters,
stuffed crab I
        think of them
as I drive inland
        through dry, red
clay, the sad, deeply
        sad South,
laden cotton
        fields, a kind of
heavy snow resting
        in the furrows. Peach
trees, pecans, turpentine and
        timber . . . overflowing
logging trucks around us
        on the road, their
load held on, it appears, by
        velocity, or
gravity, stripped trees
        that recently
were singing, that

              still chirp and
creak when
              the truck stops.

The lotus eaters don't
              travel this way
in a station
              wagon on
secondary roads
              with fighting kids
in the back. They
              spin between
continents, vacations,
              endless linen
and silk poised on
              hangers . . . .

This grimy
              car, Georgia
and more
              Georgia, and finally
rural Georgia at
              the other end of
the state, our scrubby
              town, subdivision,
then the house
              reeking like
a kennel. My old life—
              that still chirps
and creaks when the
              car stops . . . a
breath, a flame,
              a shadow.

The Bill Irwin Memorial

Every day Lane Hudson
struggles out of bed at 5:30
          and drives over to the
same spot in front of
          Winn Dixie in the
First Tuesday Mall. He does
          this in memory of his
neighbor Bill Irwin who walked
          precisely three miles every
morning for twenty years—no
          matter where he was
or what he was supposed
          to do that day. In the five
years before Lane started
          coming along,
Bill Irwin collected 843 dollars
          and 23 cents walking
the same course in the mall parking lot
          every morning, looping
back and forth like a lawn mower
          that doesn't want to
miss a patch. He taught Lane
          to go section by section,
walking the slanted lines
          of the parking spaces because that
was where people dropped
          change getting into and out
of their cars. He taught Lane
          to go to the drive-up
window at Wendy's first, though on
          Saturdays and Sundays
the pavement was picked clean
          by the guy who got there

at 5 A.M. before them. Bill showed
  Lane the couple
that rendezvoused between
  6:15 and 7:00
on Tuesday, Wednesday,
  and Thursday mornings, the
Ford pickup parking very
  close to the Mazda and
waiting for Lane and Bill
  to get out of range
to open a door. Lane never
  saw the woman's head. On
his solitary walks now, since
  Bill's death, Lane still sees
the faithful Ford and Mazda. Bill
  taught Lane about the bonanza
in the movie theater
  parking lot after the rain. In
rain, people drop their change
  from pockets, pulling out
car keys, and don't stoop to pick it up.
        One day,
  after a haul of seven cents,
Lane stopped to talk with
  Bill's widow who was
working in her garden. She
  asked if, with a take like
that, he was planning the Bill Irwin
  Memorial.
      It's hard
to be who I am
  in my new life: the cold
Midwest, the stinking
  plumes from Staley's corn
syrup factory, my husband's name

on everyone's lips. Lane changes
jobs as often as I do. He gives me
            copies of his résumé with
shadow writing beneath: "I'm a good
            ass kisser." "I'm
related to your boss." "I'll do
            anything to get a
head." And my favorite: "Please
            don't hire me."
                        I want to
apprentice myself to Lane,
            as Lane did
to Bill. To live in this
            flyover town too far
from the city to be a legitimate
            part of the "metro
area." To try patiently every day
            to get the three pennies
out of the crevice
            under the Wendy's
drive-through window. To live
            here for years, the daily
walk, to stoop to keep
            my back limber. To look
for what doesn't appear
            to be there. To look
every day for
            a kind of abundance
others overlook or disregard. To live
            that close to
the ground . . . .
                        Lane's
            got a new job, in
a town distant
            from his home. I'm not sure

30

he'll have time for
		his daily walk, since
he has to leave at six.
		When I leave
for my own new job and long
		commute ("Please
don't hire me"), Lane
		and I will settle into
another year of silence, no
		letters, e-mails, phone calls. What
we had and have when
		we're together is
too daily, too
		subtle for
wires, digits, chips, mail carriers. . . .

		Lane said to Bill that first
September, What will we do when
		winter comes and
the time changes? Bill said, We will
		walk as we do
every day at 6 A.M., just as we walk,
		even in rain, with umbrellas.
We will meet at 5:45 in every season.
		After the time change, we'll walk in
the dark. We will carry flashlights.

Charlie Butterworth Is in My Soul

Charlie Butterworth is
        in my soul, is
in my dusty venetian
        blinds, is in
the dead basil plant
        on the porch
is in the green astroturf
        on the porch's floor, is
in the standard-issue
        brown apartment carpeting
is in the peeling paint on
        the radiator in the
bathroom, the peeling linoleum
        the flaming electrical
burners, in the leftover
        Chinese food in the
refrigerator, in the whole
        house my mother would
like to dip in acid. Charlie
        Butterworth is there and
I celebrate him. He
        died of poverty
I think, that's what Mother
        said or did
he die of
        kindness Did he die
of not
        caring about
Paul Klee designer rugs
        over a polished
hardwood floor in the
        dining room He
was a lawyer but somehow

he died of drafty
rented rooms, of getting
         by, of *giving his services*
away, of the hundred poor
         people who attended his
funeral, of a wife Bernice
         who unaccountably cropped
up in the dingy
         rooms of center
city Philadelphia, radiant,
         devoted . . . . Maybe he
died of a Philadelphia
         accent
or the white dove
         on his death announcement
Charlie Butterworth!
         When I was in
boarding school, your mother picked
         me up and took
me across the
         river to her little
white house She
         gave me chicken
and dumplings and pie
         and mashed potatoes
and gravy She
         took me to a church
where the choir wore ridiculous
         pom-poms on their
heads She dragged on
         cigarettes
till the ash
         fell off She
talked and played
         cards with

the butt dangling
          from the corner of
her mouth. Aunt Kits . . . .
          Charlie
Butterworth. His brown
          eyes his kind crow's
feet, the rim of
          brown hair around
his bald head
          I wasn't supposed
to like him
          Charlie Butterworth
coming out of the faucets—
          chlorinated—in my apartment
rising off the radiator
          in waves
sluicing the path
          of the tiny silver
scar over my daughter's
          left eyebrow
My mother comes
          and says she wants
to fumigate
          call the health department
get a plastic surgeon

Hot Flash

          I live in a
hell flame like the cockscomb,
          the Chinese wool flower,
the purifying, equalizing
          fire of Isaiah. My
mother sends me
          the ivory candlesticks
Dad brought her from
          Africa in the forties
after the war. Creamy smokeless
          smokestacks
on my bedside table, the
          unspoken. But she
spoke it. She said in a
          letter, "I'm sorry
you spent so many
          years hating
me." Jesus! What can I
          say to that?

                    Lucy and
   I walk under a pumpkin-
          colored sky. Sunset bulging
against the veil
          of humidity, the resignation
of summer. We walk Sally
          on North Chauncey Street
in the murky heat. Lucy
          picks up the great curled
sheets of bark from the sycamore
          tree. Little pieces
of paper she might write
          on. Tell the story

35

of how her grandmother chased
        her in the rough
surf, yelling that she
        was drowning. Or
how they fought,
        hand to hand, over a
beach chair: "Mine!" "Mine!" I'm
        sorry you spent so many years
hating me. Only it was
        "wasted." I'm sorry
you "wasted"—No, it wasn't
        "I'm sorry." It was "It's
a shame." Shame. Yes, there,
        the candles burning
brighter now.

                My parents
        are moving into an old
people's high rise, into a "luxury
        apartment"—in which
candles are not allowed. Or
        flame, to be
precise. Ironic, isn't it?
                They enter the
purifying, equalizing
        fire of old age
and aren't allowed to
        touch it, to have it
even in the burners
        on their stove, in the
candlesticks on their
        dinner table.

                Lucy
will write her letter
        on the curling

parchment of
        sycamore, her
seventh summer on
        earth, the anxiety
she feels there. New house,
        new school; her parents
are cleaning the house
        wildly—for the
"appraiser." Does that mean
        that she will
move again? Her grandmother
        says she should be
ashamed of talking baby talk.
        She says, Don't
get too close
        to the ocean, don't
touch it.

My Mother Is Magic

My mother has a kind of magic, but she
won't let me near it. She carries a huge stone
from some ancient cornice in Malta.

She carries two ship's clocks. She walks
erect, trailing her disabilities, her oxygen apparatus, strides
to the French door and tries to open it. She

wants air, not air conditioning, ocean salt,
not sealed-off panorama. This is her new apartment,
but she won't let me in.

My mamma's dying is magic. She spends
all day thinking of the dead who went before her. Her brother
Walpole, whom she visited in Malta. Magic

Horace from Charlottesville. She didn't
love any women. I was the only one. Her mother forsook her,
took frequent sojourns at the state mental

hospital. Not appearing drunk, she removed
casseroles from the oven, set them carefully on the floor.
Mother has a picture her stepmother Eleanor painted

of her when she was seven. She had
on a red dress with white polka dots. She sat
with her ankles crossed. She told me how much

she hated that sitting. She looks fierce and
unreachable. Sallow and sad. I carry the painting
on my lap in the car,

hand carry it into her apartment.
My mother grants my daughters and me audience
one hour a day. Her lung cancer

is magic. She is riveted to her cancer.
Her runaway metabolism. She eats
     like a horse and gets thinner. Her hair grows in lush.

       My mamma, charisma. My mamma like Martha
Stewart. She smocks. She sews. She knits. She cables.
     She designs big additions on houses—

       or did. Skylights, cathedral ceilings, bay
windows with window seats. She is practically an architect.
     My mamma voodoo. She carries a slim

       black comb and five new twenty-dollar bills
in each of four tiny evening purses. She knows everything
     about tidewater: which ones are the fiddler crab,

       which ones the hermit, why
the trees stand silver and dead, like polished
     driftwood, in the swamp. That the bay water

       comes in from the ocean via
the inlet, but is also fed by freshwater springs. She knows
     to tell which parts are fresh by watching

       where the dog drinks. She knows the meaning
of "brackish." She knows how the ghost forest was made—
     when the fat cats dredged the channel for

       pleasure boats, the trees' roots were drowned.
She knows some of those fat cats. She knows high up
     in the ghost trees' branches are the messy nests

       of ospreys. The ospreys return every year,
she says, tidying slightly. On oxygen, my mother's brain's
     prodigious. She remembers everything, but she says

       it's hard to breathe. She magic
when I was a child. Her dresser, which is going to her luxury
     retirement condo, with the always

clean blue and white woven cloth on top
and the mahogany jewelry box. Rings
I occasionally glimpsed. The gold

Cleopatra necklace that was her stepmother's.
Her dresser a kind of shrine. Her whole
bedroom verboten. As I learned

every day as a child when
I opened her door during her afternoon nap
and was chased by her magic hairbrush.

Suck and Purl

The ocean sucks
    and purls
sucks and pearls
    and the whole
of Al-Anon
    runs after,
up, down, up, down,
    or they don't—
they know the minute
    it rushes
in, roils, foaming,
    all abundance,
it pulls immediately
    back, sucks hard.
The ocean took
    my daughter,
scrambled her and
    tumbled her
and then let her
    come up. My grandfather's
charisma was enormous—the
    old lady, at least
ninety, said, "We rode
    in the moonlight;
the sea was
    phosphorescent"—
suddenly awake in the
    greasy restaurant,
and his letter
    to Mother,
"Dana, darling," was
    tender like a
lover's, sad as

anything: "I am
a lonely, sick old man,
         disappointed,
disillusioned . . . ." You
         wanted to fall
in that sweet clover
         and never come out,
his solicitude for his
         daughter, her future,
his disapproval of her
         proposed marriage, his
fear she'd be a war widow
         with a "baby around her
neck," thrown on the mercy
         of the immigrant
family of "her boy."
         A year later, he
was dead of cirrhosis, leaving
         his whole estate, my mother
told me, to Lynn Somebody
         in Canada. Mother's
former guardian
         had the will
broken. At the time of
         his death,
he did not have Mother's
         address or
telephone number.

         The ocean
pulls and
         pulls hard. I come
home from visiting
         my mother, my mother's
stories, and try to

find what
of me has bobbed
        back to the foamy
surface. I look around
        my room,
my study, for pieces
        I might be
able to use. I wait
        unformed,
hovering
        like my friend
Sheila between
        bone marrows.

I swam every day
        I could while I
was visiting,
        not thinking it
could do any
        harm—ocean mother,
world-bowl full of
        beer, saline
rinse for
        my allergic
nostrils. I watched
        my father, age 76, "that boy,"
float on his back
        as I have since
I was a child.
        I never could
float like that;
        I never
could trust ocean
        that way,
I don't suppose.

In Praise of Annuals

This is the white butterfly hovering
around the flowers I just jammed into
the ground, impatient, waiting

for Shelly the garden consultant's cuttings
to bloom. This is the butterfly flitting
beautifully, communicating with me.

This is the white butterfly, fresh
from the underworld, who seems to like
my choice in cheap annuals

from Bennett Greenhouse's
Garden Day Super Sale, my "insta-garden":
orange and pink zinnias, blue salvia, yellow

treasure flowers, Chinese wool flowers, and
sweet basil. The butterfly seems to understand that
I couldn't let the sun set without making

some bright declaration. I couldn't
just slide down to the dark with Shelly's "some day"
perennials. Something about "next year"

for the sagging lungwort, the spindly columbine,
incognito primrose, creeping ajuga which
will multiply and make more of

its own low creeping purple kind.
No one has ever seen the spiky blue flowers that
are supposed to eventually be

part of the deal. Couldn't just
go down to the dark, the winter that's supposed
not to scare the hardy wintering-over

perennials—their leathery resistance,
their insistence on being all about
process and not about

consummation, always the crusty
remains of some bloom that happened in
secret—off the calendar—hanging off of them.

In my nap outfit, two layers of camisoles,
meant then not to look like camisoles, and peach
plaid flannel boxer shorts, standing

on my front porch, surveying
my hour's work, and communing with the white butterfly,
I see Shelly herself, who lives a county away,

inexplicably flapping her arm
from the passenger-side window of a passing
car. At first, I don't recognize her,

thinking her short-haired head belongs
to some young guy making fun of my outfit.
Finally, I see her grin—

has she seen my traitorous
flowers, crowding out her sagging wisps? My much
more temporary, much more gorgeous

blooms? If she has, it doesn't seem
to have distressed her. She grins hard, her obnoxious 100-
watt smile, enough to bring it all

to turgid, living, attention, to
make those dumb blue spikes of ajuga materialize, the Asiatic
lily produce, the hosta trumpet its

pale lavender news, to make silver
lavender and lamb's ear proliferate, columbine, primrose,
and hot pink lychnis

put out their velvety faces,
and the penstemon, its bearded tongue. Even the red-orange
oriental poppies *pop* up from the pathetic,

vulnerable seeds she strewed over the ground
on Monday (against what wind did she expect them
to prevail?)—Shelly who just smiled

when I told her my mother
was dead. She said, Well, she was sick, wasn't
she? Didn't she have Stage IV lung

cancer? <u>As if that solved it.</u> Shelly,
<u>still on the coffee buzz she had two days ago,</u>
<u>flapping her arm from that</u>

<u>worn maroon Honda.</u> Shelly
<u>who chums around with the plants</u>
<u>as if they were horses, slapping</u>

<u>them affectionately, pinching</u>
<u>their leaves, snapping off their "dead heads,"</u>
Shelly of the manic talking jag

can make all of summer peak
at one moment. Hence, my mother, not a white butterfly
now, stands in the garden at her house

in Virginia that she never wanted to leave,
that she gasped and lurched from that day
in June, sucking on oxygen,

her fingernails and the lower half
of her face turning blue; she stands among
her towering orange day lilies, her pink

and purple foxgloves, her black-eyed
Susans—hummingbirds hovering near her small,
dark head, the   newly cut cap of hair she died with—

and breathes.

II

Swimming at Sportsplex: February Mental Sky

"What's water but the generated soul?"
—*William Butler Yeats*

The soul was taken
by surprise, plunging
        into that glassed-
in pool in February,
        dysthymic, hyperthymic,
sex-crazed, hypomanic,
        money-throwing,
neurasthenic
        soul
rattling in its
        cage, in its
blankets and heaters
        and down
quilts, wrapped in
        layers of flannel
and wool, wearing socks,
        a fleece hat.
It plunged into
        the pool
under the cold dripping
        roof, the mauve
sky walling it in,
        making it echo,
hit its edge
        against the air's
steel wool, mohair.
        Like the last stage,
batting around
        in this daytime
twilight,

                    ricocheting off
the glass wall.
                         I can find
                    it in a pan
of water. It drips
                    from the roof
as in a hothouse,
                    the world
of exotic flowers
                    steaming,
their grave, erotic
                    faces frozen
open. . . . Bird striking
           a glass enclosure,
wall of slate
                    falling back down.
                                    First
you take the walkway
                    from the other building,
flaps of plastic on
                    either side,
freezing concrete
                    on your bare feet,
the stiff glass door. In
                    the cold, soft
air, it doesn't
                    want to get
its feet wet, its
                    body either, without
its glasses, the world
                    is smeared
with Vaseline, the
                    air is
gray, the water
                    blue-gray,

the children hardly
            visible,
have to hold the little one
            tight,
up and down the pool,
            wiggle
wiggle the legs,
            it's cold,
the black cloth of your
            swimsuit getting wetter
and wetter, taking
            on water.
This is the soul's
            element;
this is what
            you carry with you.

Making Out

This is a poem
about tenderness, about
    lips. About happening
upon a couple making
    out in Horticulture
Park and being
    surprised that
such a pointless
    act is
still being practiced. The
    slowness of
it! They're fully clothed
    and not young! Don't
look furtive or
    about to tumble
in the grass. They
    kiss—he doesn't
grab her breast and
    squeeze—they hold
each other. They pause, lean
    back, taking
in their green
    Eden. This could
hardly be called
    goal-oriented!

A fine driving mist
    comes up as
I head home—after
    I inexplicably trip
and fall headlong in
    the mulched path—maroon
blood coagulating

in the black dirt
on my knee. I was going
over the number
of dinner guests and
whether we had
enough chairs. I know
the girls will be
pleasantly horrified to see
the wound.

What I remember is
a handful, more than
a handful, of tall pines
swinging in the
breeze, balmy air and
our hammock
in the wisteria. An
apple tree loaded
down with fruit, but not
quite ready to be
picked when we left. To taste
one of those apples
from the tree in the morning—I'd
climb nearly to
the top branch. It's driving
away at 11 P.M., the girls,
the dog, the suitcases, the valuables
and shampoos in a
box next to me in the passenger
seat. The car lit
by its own headlights, and the
house light on some tree roots,
the roots of the small
maple. It's a magnolia
tree—its waxy cups

full and
tilted toward the sun—the
        fragrance, like all southern
fragrances, obscene.

        Last night, at the picnic,
Tess talked about that
        book again, *Techniques*
for Relearning Touch. ~~The guy she~~
        ~~did it with went~~
~~through all the hand-to-heart,~~
        ~~patty-cake, velvet and~~
~~feather touching, mutual~~
        ~~shampooing, and other~~
~~versions of light and heavy~~
        ~~petting with her, then~~
~~skipped right over to another~~
        ~~woman for home base.~~
~~Married her. Tess is left~~
        ~~with the book. *Red*~~
~~*light. Green light.* Circle the areas~~
        ~~where you may~~
~~not be touched with an~~
        ~~eye pencil.~~
                When
I drove away that night—after
        the girls dropped off
to sleep—I turned on raucous
        rock 'n' roll. I
wasn't thinking about making
        out, about relearning
touch. Nor leaving my husband
        only to meet
him again up the road
        when he showed up

with the moving truck. While
        the highway rushed
backward beside me,
        I was moving to the
music; I was deep inside
        the magnolia's creamy cup.

Moon Journal

When my children
were young, I hardly
        noticed you. The
baby was my moon,
        I, her sun,
and vice versa. Then
        after she stopped
nursing, the circuit
        was broken.
I got a dog—up
        went the baby
gates—I loved her
        within a
week. But
        then
she needed
        walking. Night
walks. That's
        where you came
in.

        Tonight, the
moon is gone. Stars,
        the sleeping sun's sparky
exhalations, are clear
        and close—Big
Dipper, Orion in the cold
        black sky. As if to
say, there
        are many loves,
many connections in your
        life, not just
the one you keep obsessing

about. Turning the
corner, Sally's collar jingling,
        I realize
I haven't kissed anyone
        besides my
husband in 14 years. 14
        years! Will my
lips atrophy? Then
        I remember
that last man,
        self-described
push-me, pull-you, he
        was a little
like you, moon! Another
        cradle Catholic!

                        So much I
have to learn.
        When is
the new moon (it
        seems you've
been gone for weeks);
        when is
moonrise? Moon,
        my husband
is curled in a ball
        again. He's
sad. Come on. Tell
        me about your
hopes, your alcoholic
        family, your
Irish great uncle,
        the miner, your
plans to move
        to the city,

even your loves, that
                woman
you admire who's
                avoiding
you. Tell me
                again
you like my boots.

His Hands like Warm Earth

Frank needs
love. There isn't enough
        love in the
world for Frank. I
        have to tell
him every time I go
        to the bathroom. He's
following me with
        those eyes. His
eyes say
        don't leave.
The chair
        is like
a rock and I'm
        freezing in
the air conditioning.
        The tile is
ice. The nurses have
        shut the
door. No dying
        allowed. No
needing.
        There
        isn't enough
for Peter
        either. That
much is
        apparent. I fell
in love
        with him
myself. His hands
        like warm
earth, his dark hands,

                    always on me,
casually, offhandedly. He
                    loves someone
else and
                    doesn't
notice me looking. Others
                    do, dapper Nick,
pipe fitter and chicken
                    farmer, is confused,
follows along, with
                    eyes and
hands. . . . A chain
                    of elephants
Thorny used to
                    say. Each
one nosing the
                    one ahead,
its oblivious
                    ass.
                              But
Frank and I are
                    face to
face those last
                    nights. I come
in after ten, amazed
                    at the
easy access. The walk
                    past the
gift shop down to
                    the cafeteria.
Ascent in
                    the east elevator and
then past the nurses'
                    station. Into
his room. They

don't impede
me; they don't give
            a hoot. They've
shut his
            door. Dying
is so disheartening.
                        Inside
            the sound of
cymbals, drum rolls,
            Beethoven,
Mahler, Rachmaninoff,
            Vivaldi. Inside,
silence. Air flow and
            drip of drugs
and liquid food,
            IV and
stomach tube. Frank
            is fed but
can hardly breathe. A
            gasping fish. There
isn't enough love in this
            world. His
wife who worries
            his cords
and wires, puts her
            hands here,
his chest, and there,
            his arm, his
wife of 50 years
            who irritated
him around
            the house, who
keeps him here, who
            will do anything
to keep him

here . . . .
Josh and Vicky,
            their friends
from church, swabbing
            his mouth,
moving him
            from side to
side, minding his beeping
            machine, watching
the numbers, the occasional
            nurse to empty
the catheter bag.
                        I think I see
            Peter here too,
of the warm hands; and
            Nick; and
my husband; Nick's wife;
            Peter's addict girlfriend;
Donna, Frank's water
            ballet partner; and
her young lover,
            Joey. They
are all here in this
            narrow, tiled
room, with the scrawny
            bouquet, a
rose and a pink poppy
            from Virginia's
garden, the slender
            bed, Frank
straining against its
            rails, his gown, his
feeding tube, coming
            straight out of a
hole in his bare

stomach, his
jaundiced, paper
       skin, his rasping
throat and the mouth
       that will not close,
straining against this
       life. Then that
angel . . . *with his*
       feet on the
sea and on the
       dry land.

Something Sharp and the River

Something sharp, you said,
then washed clean by the river
    to help whoever might find

    you. Anne Sexton idling her
old red '67 Cougar in her closed garage,
    stripped of her rings

    but wearing her mother's
mink coat. Sipping vodka, listening to the
    radio. How clean was it?

Shovel in the compost heap,
core sample of life, my life since
    we moved here

    two summers ago. Stains everything
it touches. Fingerprints
    on my shorts. It ate up two

    corn cobs. Miniaturized versions
of themselves, they lie side by side on my
    shovel, tiny fossils poised

on the verge of powder.
Those were our dinners, two years of good
    attempts in this strange place.

A decent burial, kneeling
in the dirt, planting seeds with my father,
    daddy longlegs in the string

    beans, baby bunnies the cat got
buried in shoeboxes up by the dogwoods.
    My father with a wheelbarrow,

spears of asparagus thrusting
through the foxtail. On the hill at dawn,
pheasants noisily rising,

creaking out of the tall
grass. I can't believe our whole conversation
was overheard by someone

at the next table!
In the Midwest, midway in the journey
of our lives. I bend

under the linden,
the mulberry, the lilac,
scoop the richest humus out.

Abigail

Blow wind
      Blow me straight
to my bones
      Blow dry my hair
Blow it off
      I won't be
needing it where
      I'm going
Lucy's little body
      leaning up
against me
      as we read
about the
      girl whose parents
keep making
      her move
Her hair's blown
      off her
scalp but she
      has the
quilt, "Abigail."
      The gale force
wind of Lucy's
      life force,
the Hoover dam,
      the gale force
wind of
      Sheila's life force
weeping alone
      in Room 3153A
bucking me
      back
wind outside batting

                battering the
house, buffeting
            the power lines,
the lights hesitate,
            we grope for the flashlight.
Blow me off
            this ship
to another
            one; blow my
hair gray, then white,
            then right off,
I'll be bald and
            naked under
a light bulb
            on 3 Central
That's the
            deck I'll land
on with
            my new hair-
do. The nurses' station
            can direct
you to my room
            Sheila's
there, Sheila!
            keeping the bed
warm, warming
            the bed
Marjorie was
            in—Debra and
Sydney shuttling in
            with goody
baskets. Sheila's
            husband baffled,
chasing their dogs
            around the suburbs

at twilight
          on his
one crutch.
          Sheila,
keep the bed warm
          for me!
I'm coming!
          Lucy's life
force knocking
          against me,
she's growing,
          multiplying
every day
          not metastisizing,
growing, getting more
          tawny, more
golden
          Wind knocks
me clean through
          Drag the girls
into the hall
          is there a
tornado, how
          will I know?
Finger my
          rosary.
Lucy wants
          to hear the
story again.

Jesus at the Help Desk

Jesus fixed my
computer. He gave me a Netscape
Communicator icon. An icon

from Jee-sus! Jesus, pronounced
Hey-Seuss, is a man from Mexico,
or Ecuador,

with freckles and a very
strange flat-iron head of black hair,
and he did not

point out to me, any
more than necessary, that I
am below idiot level

in the arcana—or
even the basicos—of computers. My own
icon so that I can get

my office e-mail from
home. He knew I needed
a lesser god to get

through this life. It has
a steering wheel on it like the
kind used on

ships. In keeping with
the term "navigator," I suppose. It
looks very like a

compass, a design feature I'm
probably the last to notice, thin spokes marking
North, South, East, West,

Northwest, Southeast,
and so on, sticking up, so handy for
keeping one's grip in a gale.

In Arles, in 1889,
van Gogh gave Gauguin an
icon, a picture

of Madame Roulin from
the bar down the street—but meant
to invoke the Virgin Mary—

holding the rope of a
cradle, though the cradle is not
visible in the picture (the picture

is meant to place *you*,
the viewer, in the cradle). To keep Gauguin *safe*,
Vincent said, in stormy

seas. Jesus knew I needed
my own intercessor. A little steering
wheel to get me

through this life, the whips
and thorns, all those *showstoppers* mixed
in with the chipper, yellow

cards of toasting and celebration,
fountains and water lilies in my Tarot future.
To help me *get through it.* This was

my mother's sole mission, I think.
To *carry on*, to dodge all the dark cards
that kept flying her way. The skull-

headed reaper on horseback
smiting all those she adored—her alcoholic
father, brothers, her heart

rent by three swords. Here, in the so-called
midpoint of my life, but certainly far
    past it, I realize van Gogh

            was a needy *pill* who gave Gauguin
everything he wanted for himself. His ardor
    was suffocating. My mother,

            just to be on the safe
side, never asked for anything . . . . It would have
    taken Einstein and Agatha

            Christie, Freud and . . .
God knows who else—God himself!—to
    figure out what

            she really wanted. I don't think
she knew. Witness her final illness
    where she still pushed

            us all away—did she
really want to be alone? Finally, when she
    was unconscious, I crept in

            and took her hand,
inscribed little crosses on her forehead.
        Her breaths, under the large

            clear oxygen mask, were harsh
and woody, coming at an unnaturally
        rapid rate. She was panting. Instinct,

            I guess you would say, the indomitable
will to live. They say Jesus waits at the end
        of a tunnel of light. I hope he

            was there, with soft hands,
for my mother, that she felt herself in Madame
    Roulin's cradle, rocked

71

by the Blessed Virgin herself. For me,
there is Hey-Suess, at the Help Desk, who
takes frantic calls all day

from people who want to
be connected, to be *in touch,* who keeps a photo
of himself and his white-gowned bride

on his desk, who looks at me wearily,
then says, "Here, I'll give you your own icon
so you can *log on."* *Get on with*

it, my mother chimes in.
But I can only utter the Breton sailors' prayer
that Vincent liked so much:

My God, protect me, my boat
is so small and your sea is
so great! Jesus looks at me blankly,

exhausted from his long day of
dispensing favors. "If you need me,"
he says without much

conviction, "just call the Help Desk."
Jesus—rhombus-headed computer jock in
Holcombe 317—he is my help.

Glass Breaking: February Meditation—
Ragdale Foundation, Lake Forest, Illinois

I wake up with glass breaking in my hips
as usual. I dreamt about New

Orleans. It wasn't magic anymore. Same
streets glistening with rain. Same, I

assume, aromatic flowers. Street names:
Feliciana, Piety, Desire. But no sense of

the exotic. Whatsoever.
A bouquet of daffodils. I

bought a bunch even though I hate
the smell and the sap makes me break

out. I bought them to remember my mother.
She was there anyway. She is always there

when I come to a new place. Uncertainty,
not knowing if I belong. Her immense presence

in all things strange, faintly
institutional. Kindergarten,

where I chased David Staskin
around the desks and wept with my face

in my skirt in the corner. First
grade, where I ached for

Jon Bauer who did not return
my affection. Who checked, consistently,

the "no" box in my little
love query notes. "U"'s—Unsatisfactories—

in "self-control" on every report
card through elementary school—tempted

by boys to talk, then caught. Nerdy, intellectual
junior high, bangs in my face, big metally

braces. Boarding school in ninth grade, the
place she spent five years, starting

at age eleven. She was there
as she is here, thirty years

later. I was standing before a white portico
at St. Margaret's, sobbing, as my brother, who'd

driven six hours to deliver me,
left to drive home. Glass breaking

in my hips. Here, in Lake Forest,
the guilt of the rich. I haven't

seen it in a while. But how
familiar, my family assembled

in their ties and blazers at dinner.
On the streets of this little town, Mercedes Benzes

and Lexuses, Argyle sweaters and
socks (double indemnity: cashmere!). Penny

loafers. The same bald heads with
the monk's rim of brown hair. Bred in,

apparently, the pattern baldness. Glass
breaking in my knees, jaw, third cervical

vertebra, but *mostly* my hips. I miss my
children. Are Eleanor's hands getting

chapped? At night I rubbed the cream in
deep. We talked about our days as she

dropped off. The first month we took
turns sobbing over what we

missed about Georgia. And Lucy. Who's parting
her hair carefully, making her "pink tails"?

Lucy, I try to focus, not to hurt.
All the editors hate the perky, little

enjambed lines. They especially
write to tell me so. They're tormented by the

expensive white space over on the right. This is for you,
friends. No more perk. Now publish me so

I can get a decent job and not have
to write quizzes for Scholastic Books. I have holes

in my a) pants, b) socks, c) skirts,
d) underwear, e) all of the above. Oops,

there should be only one correct answer. And
we wonder why college students can't argue

from a text. They saw a text
once and then were quizzed on what was

"memorable." They never lay down next to
it and let it in their pores. "Names, dates, places,

and other numbers are not memorable for the
reader." "Avoid questions based on inferences."

Five or more of the multiple choice questions
must contain "because." "Why"

also satisfies the "because" requirement.
Two to five questions in "cloze" format,

fill-in-the-blank. "Answer stems" around six
words. One to three vocabulary questions, two to

five question marks. The men indistinguishable in their overcoats,
milling the Lake Forest train station. A child could mistake any one

for her daddy as I did in suburban Philadelphia.
That's it. It's the fifties.

It's Cheever-land. The men return from their hard
days in the city, their bag lunches,

to the waiting aprons. Pipes, crossed legs,
deep, abiding entitlement. Yes. There.

Where? Oh yes, it was New Orleans, and
it was night and the street lamps

illuminated the damp streets,
Piety, Feliciana, Desire,

Tchoupitoulas, Dauphine, Dante,
Constance, Toulouse, St. Charles.

"Use actions instead of details." "By
paraphrasing and blending information, you

can easily avoid copyright infringement."
No details, no quotes, no

specifics, no names for things, no
motives, no character development . . . .

Forced hyacinths in the breezeway. I hate them
worse than the daffodils. Sickening. My

mother in pumps and beige cashmere sweater, looking
out at the Pennsylvania gloom,

waiting out the days. In my dream, it was New Orleans,
night, and gas lamps

illuminated damp streets. The streets were
the same ones I had a) walked down

beer in hand, b) glided down stoned on hash, c) slid
down pulverized from sex, d) ridden on at 4 A.M.

coming home from work on my ten-speed. In dream, those streets
as bald as daylight, as the lights switched

on after closing and the nickels counted.
Piety, Desire, Constance,

Louisa, Feliciana, Bartholomew,
Gallia, Montague . . . "Names,

dates, places, and other numbers
are not memorable for the reader" . . .

Gravier, Amelia, Acacia, Dumaine,
Burgundy, Chartres, Tchoupitoulas,

all these years carried in my head, my body. It was night
and the streetlights illuminated the damp

streets, night flowers opening
in secret, their cloying scent. In February! Openly sexual.

Not my mother's forced narcissi. I felt *away* when I lived
there, a thousand miles from Philadelphia. I was in some

kind of let-it-all-hang-out Latin/European
heaven. The dream says that's over now. Like my mother,

I'm looking out a frost-encrusted window waiting
for spring. And the night flowers opening in secret,

their cloying scent: *Feliciana, Hope, Piety, Desire.*

Fugue in Summer: Don on the Sofa Again

The ground is sere;
it would take a jackhammer
        to open
a space for a petunia
        and, still,
it hasn't rained
        in ten days—so
much rain,
        then nothing.
In the cloudy, milky
        light
Lucy and I
        pass over the
baked clay
        with our hoes,
our poles. Lucy pokes
        fire ant enclaves,
I pull back
        Eleanor's clover which
encroaches
        on the garden's edge—
home of four-leaf
        clovers, now a nest
underneath for
        families of slugs.
In the twilight,
        so still and hot,
of waiting for
        something to happen,
an event of weather,
        an "impulse,"
oddly, something
        does—the eerie off-key

tinkle of the ice
        cream truck and Lucy's
running;
        I scream, *We've got
to get some money!
        and we run in
for it, waking
        Don, and out
again, to the street.

The Water Table

       Harold's 15-year-old daughter
knew about two safeties
      and unlocked them
but didn't know about
      the third—a
hidden pin—
      and couldn't get the
gun to fire. Harold's
      blue-eyed, intense
daughter who now lives
      in California,
23, with 7 years sobriety.
      You can tell he
doesn't want to let her
      go back, but
how can he hold her, only 4
      years sober
himself? The water
      of life,
Father John says, cleans
      us, heals us;
we are dipped down in
      it, allowed
to die, and then
      brought back up
without that original
      sin that
makes us so unpleasant.
      Devil,
get thee behind me.
      The water has
to be alive, moving,
      hence the pond

Monsignor Regan had dredged
        behind the rectory
for baptisms 20 years
        ago. Now,
retired, he dips in
        and out of
the hospital, out of
        lucidity, but perfectly
clear, he gushes,
        "You and
your husband have
        so much
and those girls . . . .
        He said he
wants a divorce?" Then,
        with a laugh,
"Those are only
        words." Each
time I see him, I drink
        him up, afraid I'll soon be
left with his
        New Testament
translated by Knox
        and my spotty
memory. Harold says when
        Jessica goes back
to California, she'll
        start again at college,
aim for something
        to do with
emergency medicine,
        and I remember
what Ann said, that
        emergency work is
a typical career

choice of "children
from dysfunctional
          families." She
told me about a man who's gone so
          far as to become
a salvage diver, an
          underwater
EMT; we laughed,
          thinking of Freud
and the great unconscious,
          to be able
to swim in it
          every day, and
save people. Jessica
          could save anyone,
I think—she saved
          me a few
weeks ago when
          I thought
I would sink, my
          marriage set
adrift on the
          great
change of life—I can't
          believe they call
it that. Does every woman
          fall asleep and
wake back up in
          a different life?

Every week
          for two weeks now
Father John
          has prayed for
the teenage lovers, Andrea

and Jeff, who
died in a stall
in the Ladies Room
at Central High. He prays,
his voice
breaking as though he
too would break. And we
picture them
curled there. Not as
they were—the janitor
who found them,
after all, had
to be
hospitalized afterward—but as
we'd like them
to be, two babes
in the wood
who lay down in
a grassy glade
and didn't get back
up.
We come out from mass,
this is Georgia,
January 17,
to a
spring rain. John,
my brother,
tells us at dinner
that what
will get us in the end
will be
the water table—all those
pesticides
have to eventually
go somewhere,

that pesky original
        sin, like
the Cat in the Hat's
        pink bath-
tub ring.
        Somewhere
awaits the savior
        or little
cat "Z"
        who, in one
decisive blow, one
        electric jolt, one
VOOM, will
        clean it up.
                                I
saw a painting called
        The Fifth Step
once, a black velvet background
        with paint
squiggles and other detritus
        all over it, the great
unconscious unburdening
        itself—
the guy who painted
        it went
back out. I saw him
        at a coffee
shop one day, flushed
        and shaking, faking
it. Carl, I think his
        name was,
and I haven't thought of
        him in years.
He wore white painter's pants
        and was so

intent and charming in
          meetings. I didn't
fall in love with him,
          though. I was
a thousand percent in
          love with my
husband; there was
          a kind of harmony
then, my sins were fitting
          in well,
I guess, in a way
          they simply
aren't now. Money
          & children &
mortgages hadn't raised
          their heads.
Hot flashes, car
          wrecks, marriage
counseling and carpenter
          bees, killer wisteria,
runaway ivy and the ten
          deep, muddy
holes Sally has dug
          in the
backyard. Mammogram
          callbacks, bone density
studies, and borderline
          ovarian function,
St. John's Wort, memory
          enhancement
pills and the 5-foot
          laundry tower. Sheila's
bone marrow transplant and
          subsequent graft vs.
host disease. Inappropriate

crushes on
gas station
        attendants,
convenience store
        clerks, sweaty intramural
basketball players
        at the gym. God, Jesus,
Mary, and all
        the saints,
I can't carry this
        mess, *my*
mess any longer,
        dip me
down in that sprinkler,
        hose, puddle, whatever's
handy, that I might
        be cleaned, that
we might be
        cleaned,
healed of our
        bitter resentments,
our *spiritual pride,*
        our *doubt, distress,*
our *fear of death,* that
        we might be
healed of our
        messy
trespasses.

Beautiful Motion

He said, I came so that
you could have life and have
it to the full. *And then
the fish Win caught hightailed
it away, a voluptuous
motion, out of the shallows, into
the depths.* He said
it nearly every Sunday
and then
hightailed it away, took
off his cassock, his
collar, his surplice, his
stole, so that
he could have life and have it
to the full. *Win
swished the fish back and forth
in the water, holding
its mouth wide open so
that it could
get its strength back.* I got
a bolt of electricity
every week when
he gave me
the communion wafer. The
Body of Christ
drilling right through me
down to my toes. No
one ever denied it
was like
sex. The tomatoes overflow
the self-serve
organic farm stand

on Weatogue
Road. I stop in to sniff
        the vegetables,
the faint smell
        of compost. Ripe
tomatoes take up the whole
        counter almost
crowding out the money
        tin. Sunflowers,
gladioli, onions, zucchini,
        summer squash, beets,
potatoes and green beans. Lettuce. I
        banged my head
so hard on the floor, I
        nearly cracked
my skull. We'd moved
        from the bed
for better torque. I screamed
        my lungs out, having
life to the full. My husband's
        sweaty body
over me, sluicing me with
        water. There wasn't anything
left then, we spent it
        all, our bad backs, and
our bad knees, our respective melancholias,
        our skin problems, our
career schticks went up in
        smoke. The tiny
voices of our children
        far away. Outside the
window, the mountains were sad, as all
        mountains are,
especially the green ones
        that turn to blue. They

wept and grieved, even
        as we screamed
our desperate joy. They
        keened. The old people,
my husband's parents, are getting
        so frail. *After you leave*
today, you may not
        see them ever
again. My daughter's plaintive goodbye
        letter, left for her
grandmother on her dresser, "I hope
        your dizzy spells get
better," and to retarded Uncle
        Mike who cannot
read: "Keep rockin'
        to the CD I gave
you." The mountains
        with their steady,
measured sobbing, the tomatoes
        multiplying and
ripening, Father John with
        his backaches and
his migraines, off to California,
        finally having
it to the full. My screams. Don's
        sweat soaking
the fifties shag carpet on
        the floor of his
parents' bedroom. Win's
        large-mouthed bass nearly
flipping from his hands
        as we snap the
picture. Then, in the water,
        the beautiful
motion, away.

NOTES

"November 15, Before the Frost" is for J.D.G.

"The Bill Irwin Memorial" is for Lane Hudson, with my thanks.

The title "Suck and Purl" is taken from a line in "Tomatoes," the second poem in a two-part sequence, "Farm Poems," by Lisa Russ (Spaar) in *Cellar* (Charlottesville, Va.: Alderman Press, 1983).

"In Praise of Annuals" is in memory of my mother, Daingerfield (Dana) Davis Roeser (1925–2002).

"His Hands like Warm Earth" is dedicated to the memory of F. H. (1925–2000). The italicized lines at the end of the poem are from Revelation 10:5 (trans. Ronald Knox).

A NOTE ON THE AUTHOR

Dana Roeser grew up in the Philadelphia area and was educated at Tulane University (B.A.), the University of Virginia (M.A., M.F.A.), and the University of Utah. Her poems have appeared in the *Iowa Review, Virginia Quarterly Review, Massachusetts Review, Indiana Review, Another Chicago Magazine, Northwest Review, Pool, Shade,* and others, as well as on *Poetry Daily.* She has received fellowships from the Virginia Center for the Creative Arts and the Ragdale Foundation. She teaches at Butler University in Indianapolis and lives with her husband and two daughters in West Lafayette, Indiana.

A NOTE ON THE PRIZE

The Samuel French Morse Poetry Prize was established in 1983 by the Northeastern University Department of English in order to honor Professor Morse's distinguished career as teacher, scholar, and poet. The members of the prize committee are Francis C. Blessington, Joseph deRoche, Victor Howes, Stuart Peterfreund, Guy Rotella, and Ellen Scharfenberg.